M000012297

To:

_____

From:

_____

Date:

_____

Message:

_____

_____

_____

Published by Christian Art Publishers
PO Box 1599, Vereeniging, 1930, RSA

© 2019
First edition 2019

Designed by Christian Art Publishers

Images used under license from Shutterstock.com

Printed in China

ISBN 978-1-4321-2909-5

Promises
from God
— FOR —
Women

**CHRISTIAN ART
PUBLISHERS**

Contents

1. The unfading beauty of a
   gentle and quiet spirit 7
2. She speaks with wisdom 11
3. Clothed with strength and dignity 15
4. Worth far more than rubies 19
5. Above all these things put on love 23
6. Trust in the Lord with all your heart 27
7. Do not give up 31
8. A kindhearted woman gains honor 35
9. A woman who fears the
   Lord is to be praised 39
10. Hope in the Lord! 43
11. The faithful love of the
    Lord never ends! 47
12. Grace and peace be yours
    in abundance 51
13. Do not be anxious about anything 55
14. The Lord your God will be with you 59

15. Rest in the shadow of the Almighty 63

16. The joy of the Lord is your strength 67

17. Better to be patient than powerful 71

18. The prayer of a righteous person
    is powerful and effective 75

19. Whatever you do, do it all
    for the glory of God 79

20. The plans of the Lord stand
    firm forever 83

21. Give thanks to the Lord! 87

22. The Lord will guide you always 91

23. Blessed is the one who
    trusts in the Lord 95

24. The Lord comforts His people 99

25. Clothe yourselves with humility 103

26. The word of God is alive and active 107

27. Set your mind on things above 111

28. Don't copy the customs
    of this world 115

29. Draw near to God 119

30. Our God is a God who saves 123

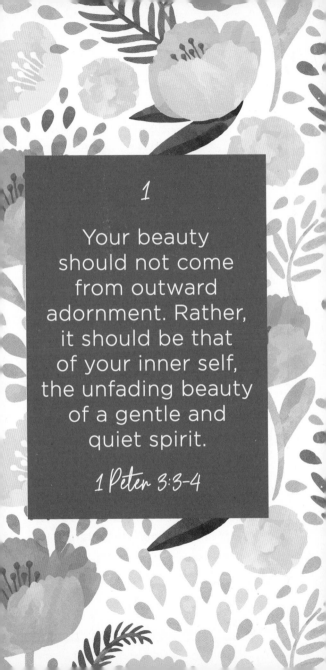

1

Your beauty should not come from outward adornment. Rather, it should be that of your inner self, the unfading beauty of a gentle and quiet spirit.

1 Peter 3:3-4

"The Lord does not look at the things people look at. People look at the outward appearance, but the Lord looks at the heart."
1 SAMUEL 16:7 NIV

He has made everything beautiful in its time.
ECCLESIASTES 3:11 NIV

I praise You because I am fearfully and wonderfully made; Your works are wonderful, I know that full well.
PSALM 139:14 NIV

Know that the Lord is God. It is He who made us, and we are His; we are His people, the sheep of His pasture.
PSALM 100:3 NIV

We are God's masterpiece. He has created us anew in Christ Jesus, so we can do the good things He planned for us long ago.
EPHESIANS 2:10 NLT

"So why do you worry about clothing? Consider the lilies of the field, how they grow: they neither toil nor spin; and yet I say to you that even Solomon in all his glory was not arrayed like one of these."

MATTHEW 6:28-29 NKJV

God created human beings in His own image. In the image of God He created them; male and female He created them.

GENESIS 1:27 NLT

Those who look to Him are radiant, and their faces shall never be ashamed.

PSALM 34:5 ESV

Do you not know that your bodies are temples of the Holy Spirit, who is in you, whom you have received from God? You are not your own; you were bought at a price. Therefore honor God with your bodies.

1 CORINTHIANS 6:19-20 NIV

Like a gold ring in a pig's snout is a beautiful woman who shows no discretion.
PROVERBS 11:22 NIV

How beautiful on the mountains are the feet of the messenger who brings good news, the good news of peace and salvation, the news that the God of Israel reigns!
ISAIAH 52:7 NLT

Physical training is good, but training for godliness is much better, promising benefits in this life and in the life to come.
1 TIMOTHY 4:8 NLT

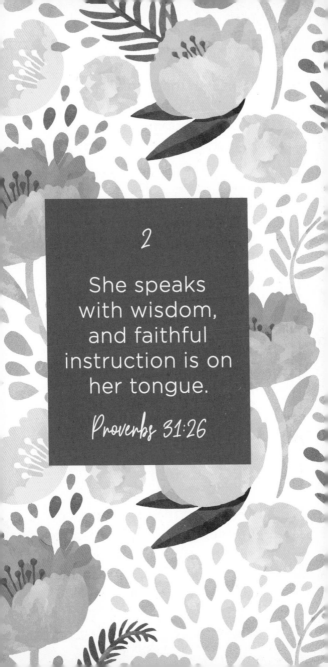

2

She speaks
with wisdom,
and faithful
instruction is on
her tongue.

Proverbs 31:26

The wisdom that comes from heaven is first of all pure; then peace-loving, considerate, submissive, full of mercy and good fruit, impartial and sincere.
JAMES 3:17 NIV

Wisdom is sweet to your soul. If you find it, you will have a bright future, and your hopes will not be cut short.
PROVERBS 24:14 NLT

For the LORD gives wisdom; from His mouth come knowledge and understanding.
PROVERBS 2:6 NIV

If you need wisdom, ask our generous God, and He will give it to you. He will not rebuke you for asking.
JAMES 1:5 NLT

The law of the LORD is perfect, refreshing the soul. The statutes of the LORD are trustworthy, making wise the simple.
PSALM 19:7 NIV

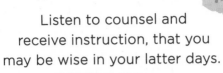

Listen to counsel and
receive instruction, that you
may be wise in your latter days.
PROVERBS 19:20 NKJV

"To God belong wisdom
and power; counsel and
understanding are His."
JOB 12:13 NIV

God gives wisdom, knowledge,
and joy to those who please Him.
ECCLESIASTES 2:26 NLT

By wisdom a house is built, and by
understanding it is established;
by knowledge the rooms are filled
with all precious and pleasant riches.
PROVERBS 24:3-4 ESV

Praise the name of God forever
and ever, for He has all wisdom and
power. He gives wisdom to the wise
and knowledge to the scholars,
DANIEL 2:20-21 NLT

The fear of the LORD is the
beginning of wisdom,
and knowledge of the
Holy One is understanding.
PROVERBS 9:10 NIV

Wisdom will enter your
heart, and knowledge
will fill you with joy.
PROVERBS 2:10 NLT

Do not forsake wisdom,
and she will protect you;
love her, and she will
watch over you.
PROVERBS 4:6 NIV

Instruct the wise and they
will be wiser still; teach
the righteous and they will
add to their learning.
PROVERBS 9:9 NIV

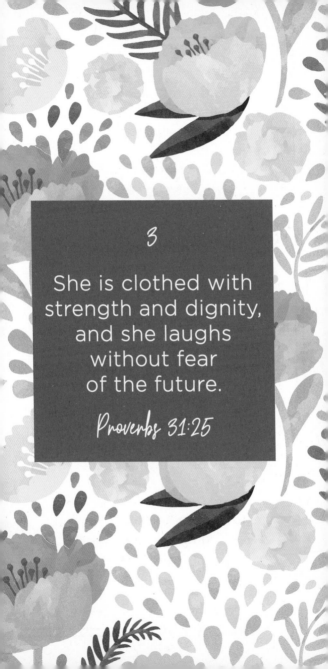

3

She is clothed with
strength and dignity,
and she laughs
without fear
of the future.

Proverbs 31:25

God is our refuge and strength,
an ever-present help in trouble.
PSALM 46:1 NIV

I can do all things through Christ
who strengthens me.
PHILIPPIANS 4:13 NKJV

God arms me with strength,
and He makes my way perfect.
He makes me as surefooted as a
deer, enabling me to stand on
mountain heights. He trains my
hands for battle; He strengthens
my arm to draw a bronze bow.
PSALM 18:32-34 NLT

The LORD gives strength to
His people; the LORD blesses
His people with peace.
PSALM 29:11 NIV

"My grace is sufficient for you,
for My strength is made
perfect in weakness."
2 CORINTHIANS 12:9 NKJV

The Sovereign Lord is my
strength; He makes my feet like
the feet of a deer, He enables
me to tread on the heights.
HABAKKUK 3:19 NIV

"I will seek the lost, and I will
bring back the strayed, and I
will bind up the injured, and
I will strengthen the weak."
EZEKIEL 34:16 ESV

The Lord is faithful, and
He will strengthen and
protect you from the evil one.
2 THESSALONIANS 3:3 NIV

"Do not fear, for I am with you;
do not be dismayed, for I am your
God. I will strengthen you and
help you; I will uphold you with
My righteous right hand."
ISAIAH 41:10 NIV

My health may fail, and my
spirit may grow weak, but
God remains the strength of my
heart; He is mine forever.
PSALM 73:26 NLT

"In repentance and rest is
your salvation, in quietness
and trust is your strength."
ISAIAH 30:15 NIV

The LORD is my strength and my
song; He has given me victory.
PSALM 118:14 NLT

The LORD is my light and my
salvation; whom shall I fear?
The LORD is the strength
of my life; of whom
shall I be afraid?
PSALM 27:1 NKJV

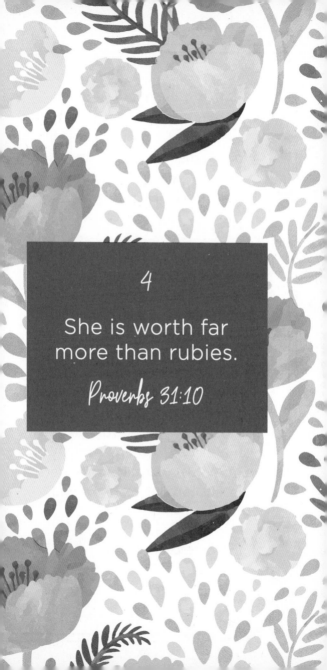

4

She is worth far
more than rubies.

Proverbs 31:10

"Are not two sparrows sold for a penny? Yet not one of them will fall to the ground outside your Father's care. So don't be afraid; you are worth more than many sparrows."

MATTHEW 10:29-31 NIV

"God so loved the world that He gave His only begotten Son, that whoever believes in Him should not perish but have everlasting life."

JOHN 3:16 NKJV

"Look at the lilies and how they grow. They don't work or make their clothing, yet Solomon in all his glory was not dressed as beautifully as they are. And if God cares so wonderfully for flowers, He will certainly care for you."

LUKE 12:27-28 NLT

"You did not choose Me, but I chose you."

JOHN 15:16 ESV

The Lord your God has
chosen you to be a people for
Himself, a special treasure above all
the peoples on the face of the earth.
DEUTERONOMY 7:6 NKJV

"Before I formed you in the womb
I knew you, before you were born
I set you apart; I appointed you
as a prophet to the nations."
JEREMIAH 1:5 NIV

God decided in advance to adopt
us into His own family by bringing
us to Himself through Jesus Christ.
This is what He wanted to do,
and it gave Him great pleasure.
EPHESIANS 1:5 NLT

See how very much our Father
loves us, for He calls us His children,
and that is what we are!
1 JOHN 3:1 NLT

Know that the Lord has set apart
His faithful servant for Himself.
PSALM 4:3 NIV

You are a chosen people,
a royal priesthood,
a holy nation,
God's special possession.
1 PETER 2:9 NIV

You have been set apart as
holy to the LORD your God, and
He has chosen you from all the
nations of the earth to be
His own special treasure.
DEUTERONOMY 14:2 NLT

He is Lord of lords and
King of kings; and those who
are with Him are called,
chosen, and faithful.
REVELATION 17:14 NKJV

5

Above all these
things put on love,
which is the bond
of perfection.

Colossians 3:14

"I am giving you a new commandment: Love each other. Just as I have loved you, you should love each other."
JOHN 13:34 NLT

Anyone who loves God must also love their brother and sister.
1 JOHN 4:21 NIV

Love prospers when a fault is forgiven, but dwelling on it separates close friends.
PROVERBS 17:9 NLT

There is no fear in love; but perfect love casts out fear.
1 JOHN 4:18 NKJV

Love your neighbor as yourself.
LEVITICUS 19:18 NIV

Live a life filled with love, following the example of Christ.
EPHESIANS 5:2 NLT

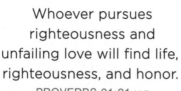

Whoever pursues
righteousness and
unfailing love will find life,
righteousness, and honor.
PROVERBS 21:21 NLT

Love is patient, love is kind.
It does not envy, it does
not boast, it is not proud.
1 CORINTHIANS 13:4 NIV

Do everything in love.
1 CORINTHIANS 16:14 NIV

This is love: not that we
loved God, but that He loved
us and sent His Son as an
atoning sacrifice for our sins.
1 JOHN 4:10 NIV

Let love and faithfulness never
leave you; bind them around
your neck, write them on
the tablet of your heart.
PROVERBS 3:3 NIV

Love the LORD your God with all your heart and with all your soul and with all your strength.
DEUTERONOMY 6:5 NIV

If we love each other, God lives in us, and His love is brought to full expression in us.
1 JOHN 4:12 NLT

Love never fails.
1 CORINTHIANS 13:8 NKJV

These three remain: faith, hope and love. But the greatest of these is love.
1 CORINTHIANS 13:13 NIV

Love covers over a multitude of sins.
1 PETER 4:8 NIV

6

Trust in the LORD with all your heart, and do not lean on your own understanding. In all your ways acknowledge Him, and He will make straight your paths.

Proverbs 3:5-6

"I tell you the truth, if you had faith even as small as a mustard seed, you could say to this mountain, 'Move from here to there,' and it would move. Nothing would be impossible."
MATTHEW 17:20 NLT

Be on your guard; stand firm in the faith; be courageous; be strong.
1 CORINTHIANS 16:13 NIV

Now faith is the substance of things hoped for, the evidence of things not seen.
HEBREWS 11:1 NKJV

Because of Christ and our faith in Him, we can now come boldly and confidently into God's presence.
EPHESIANS 3:12 NLT

In all circumstances take up the shield of faith, with which you can extinguish all the flaming darts of the evil one.
EPHESIANS 6:16 ESV

Make every effort to
supplement your faith
with virtue, and virtue with
knowledge, and knowledge with
self-control, and self-control with
steadfastness, and steadfastness
with godliness, and godliness
with brotherly affection, and
brotherly affection with love.
2 PETER 1:5-7 ESV

Faith comes from hearing the
message, and the message is heard
through the word about Christ.
ROMANS 10:17 NIV

Without faith it is impossible to
please Him, for he who comes
to God must believe that He is,
and that He is a rewarder of
those who diligently seek Him.
HEBREWS 11:6 NKJV

For I can do everything through
Christ, who gives me strength.
PHILIPPIANS 4:13 NLT

Everyone who believes that Jesus is the Christ has been born of God, and everyone who loves the Father loves whoever has been born of Him.

1 JOHN 5:1 ESV

I have fought the good fight, I have finished the race, I have kept the faith.

2 TIMOTHY 4:7 NIV

"Anyone who believes and is baptized will be saved. But anyone who refuses to believe will be condemned."

MARK 16:16 NLT

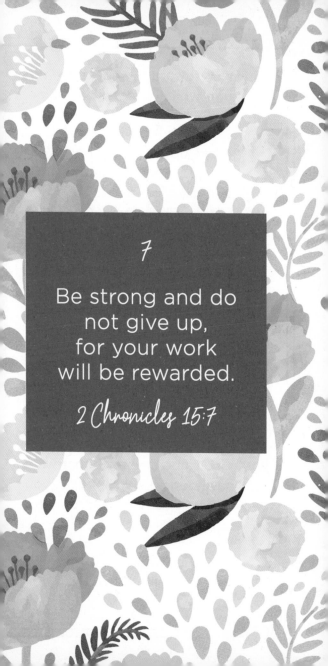

7

Be strong and do
not give up,
for your work
will be rewarded.

2 Chronicles 15:7

I press on toward the goal to win the prize for which God has called me.
PHILIPPIANS 3:14 NIV

Take up your positions;
stand firm and see the
deliverance the LORD
will give you.
2 CHRONICLES 20:17 NIV

We have come to share in Christ,
if indeed we hold our original
conviction firmly to the very end.
HEBREWS 3:14 NIV

Let us not become weary in doing
good, for at the proper time we will
reap a harvest if we do not give up.
GALATIANS 6:9 NIV

You need to persevere so that when
you have done the will of God, you
will receive what He has promised.
HEBREWS 10:36 NIV

"He who endures to the
end shall be saved."
MATTHEW 24:13 NKJV

Always give yourselves
fully to the work of the Lord,
because you know that your
labor in the Lord is not in vain.
1 CORINTHIANS 15:58 NIV

Blessed is the one who perseveres
under trial because, having stood
the test, that person will receive
the crown of life that the Lord has
promised to those who love Him.
JAMES 1:12 NIV

Consider it pure joy, my brothers
and sisters, whenever you face
trials of many kinds, because you
know that the testing of your
faith produces perseverance.
JAMES 1:2-3 NIV

We also glory in our sufferings,
because we know that suffering
produces perseverance;
perseverance, character;
and character, hope.
ROMANS 5:3-4 NIV

Let us run with endurance the
race God has set before us.
We do this by keeping our eyes
on Jesus, the champion who
initiates and perfects our faith.
HEBREWS 12:1-2 NLT

Make every effort to confirm
your calling and election.
For if you do these things,
you will never stumble, and
you will receive a rich welcome
into the eternal kingdom of
our Lord and Savior Jesus Christ.
2 PETER 1:10-11 NIV

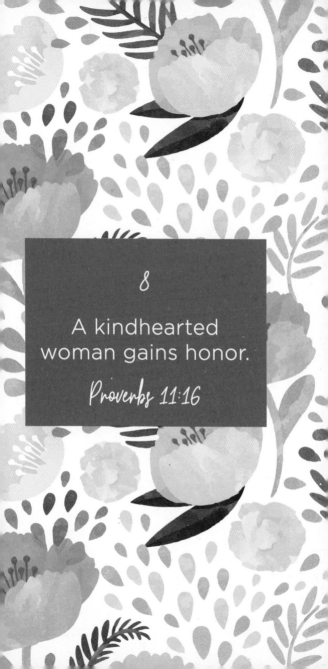

8

A kindhearted
woman gains honor.

Proverbs 11:16

Never tire of doing what is good.
2 THESSALONIANS 3:13 NIV

Anxiety weighs down the heart,
but a kind word cheers it up.
PROVERBS 12:25 NIV

"In everything, do to others what
you would have them do to you."
MATTHEW 7:12 NIV

Tell the LORD how thankful
you are, because He is kind
and always merciful.
PSALM 118:1 CEV

Look after each other so
that none of you fails to
receive the grace of God.
HEBREWS 12:15 NLT

Those who are kind benefit
themselves, but the cruel
bring ruin on themselves.
PROVERBS 11:17 NIV

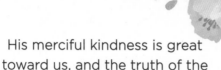

His merciful kindness is great
toward us, and the truth of the
LORD endures forever.
PSALM 117:2 NKJV

It is a sin to despise one's
neighbor, but blessed is the one
who is kind to the needy.
PROVERBS 14:21 NIV

Be kind and compassionate to
one another, forgiving each other,
just as in Christ God forgave you.
EPHESIANS 4:32 NIV

Whoever is kind to the poor lends
to the LORD, and He will reward
them for what they have done.
PROVERBS 19:17 NIV

Whoever oppresses the poor
shows contempt for their Maker,
but whoever is kind to the
needy honors God.
PROVERBS 14:31 NIV

The fruit of the Spirit is love, joy, peace, patience, kindness, goodness, faithfulness, gentleness and self-control.

GALATIANS 5:22-23 NIV

I will tell of the kindnesses of the Lord, the deeds for which He is to be praised, according to all the Lord has done for us.

ISAIAH 63:7 NIV

Make sure that nobody pays back wrong for wrong, but always strive to do what is good for each other and for everyone else.

1 THESSALONIANS 5:15 NIV

"If anyone gives even a cup of cold water to one of these little ones who is My disciple, truly I tell you, that person will certainly not lose their reward."

MATTHEW 10:42 NIV

9

Charm is deceptive, and beauty is fleeting; but a woman who fears the LORD is to be praised.

Proverbs 31:30

Since we are receiving a Kingdom
that is unshakable, let us be thankful
and please God by worshiping
Him with holy fear and awe.
For our God is a devouring fire.
HEBREWS 12:28-29 NLT

Be sure to fear the LORD and serve Him
faithfully with all your heart; consider
what great things He has done for you.
1 SAMUEL 12:24 NIV

From the throne
came a voice saying,
"Praise our God, all you
His servants, you who
fear Him, small and great."
REVELATION 19:5 ESV

Honor all people. Love
the brotherhood. Fear God.
1 PETER 2:17 NKJV

"Do not curse the deaf or
put a stumbling block in
front of the blind, but fear your
God. I am the LORD."
LEVITICUS 19:14 NIV

How joyful are those who
fear the LORD – all who
follow His ways! You will enjoy
the fruit of your labor. How joyful
and prosperous you will be!
PSALM 128:1-2 NLT

Reverence for the LORD is pure,
lasting forever. The laws of the
LORD are true; each one is fair.
PSALM 19:9 NLT

The fear of the LORD is the
beginning of wisdom; a good
understanding have all those
who do His commandments.
His praise endures forever.
PSALM 111:10 NKJV

The LORD takes pleasure in those
who fear Him, in those who
hope in His steadfast love.
PSALM 147:11 ESV

The angel of the LORD encamps
all around those who fear Him,
and delivers them.
PSALM 34:7 NKJV

Whoever fears the LORD has a
secure fortress, and for their
children it will be a refuge.
The fear of the LORD is a fountain
of life, turning a person from
the snares of death.
PROVERBS 14:26-27 NIV

Fear God and keep His
commandments, for this
is the whole duty of man.
ECCLESIASTES 12:13 ESV

Let the whole world fear
the LORD, and let everyone
stand in awe of Him. For
when He spoke, the world
began! It appeared at
His command.
PSALM 33:8-9 NLT

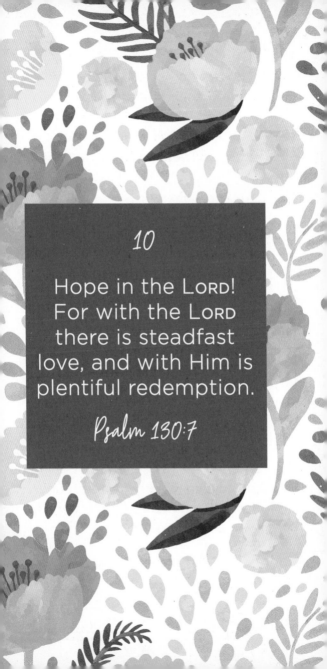

10

Hope in the LORD!
For with the LORD
there is steadfast
love, and with Him is
plentiful redemption.

Psalm 130:7

Those who hope in the LORD will
renew their strength. They will
soar on wings like eagles; they
will run and not grow weary,
they will walk and not be faint.
ISAIAH 40:31 NIV

May the God of hope fill you with
all joy and peace as you trust in Him,
so that you may overflow with hope
by the power of the Holy Spirit.
ROMANS 15:13 NIV

Having hope will give you
courage. You will be protected
and will rest in safety.
JOB 11:18 NLT

We have this hope as an anchor
for the soul, firm and secure. It
enters the inner sanctuary behind
the curtain, where our forerunner,
Jesus, has entered on our behalf.
HEBREWS 6:19-20 NIV

Blessed are those whose hope is
in the LORD their God.
PSALM 146:5 NIV

Hope will not lead to
disappointment. For we know
how dearly God loves us, because
He has given us the Holy Spirit to fill
our hearts with His love.
ROMANS 5:5 NLT

The eye of the LORD is on those
who fear Him, on those who
hope in His steadfast love.
PSALM 33:18 ESV

My help comes from the LORD,
who made heaven and earth!
PSALM 121:2 NLT

I pray that the eyes of your
heart may be enlightened in order
that you may know the hope to
which He has called you.
EPHESIANS 1:18-19 NIV

I saw the Lord always before me ...
therefore my heart is glad
and my tongue rejoices;
my body also will live in hope.
ACTS 2:25-26 NIV

The needy shall not always be forgotten, and the hope of the poor shall not perish forever.
PSALM 9:18 ESV

Hope deferred makes the heart sick, but a dream fulfilled is a tree of life.
PROVERBS 13:12 NLT

Why, my soul,
are you downcast?
Why so disturbed within me?
Put your hope in God,
for I will yet praise Him,
my Savior and my God.
PSALM 43:5 NIV

The LORD takes pleasure in those who fear Him, in those who hope in His mercy.
PSALM 147:11 NKJV

11

The faithful love of the LORD never ends! His mercies never cease. Great is His faithfulness; His mercies begin afresh each morning.

Lamentations 3:22-23

Give thanks to the God of gods.
His love endures forever.
PSALM 136:2 NIV

"I have loved you even as the Father
has loved Me. Remain in My love."
JOHN 15:9 NLT

Greater love has no one than this: to
lay down one's life for one's friends.
JOHN 15:13 NIV

See how very much our Father
loves us, for He calls us His children,
and that is what we are!
1 JOHN 3:1 NLT

For I am convinced that neither
death nor life, neither angels nor
demons, neither the present nor
the future, nor any powers,
neither height nor depth,
nor anything else in all creation,
will be able to separate us
from the love of God.
ROMANS 8:38-39 NIV

"I am the good shepherd.
The good shepherd lays
down His life for the sheep."
JOHN 10:11 NIV

"I lavish unfailing love for a thousand
generations on those who love Me
and obey My commands."
DEUTERONOMY 5:10 NLT

"I have loved you with an
everlasting love; I have drawn
you with unfailing kindness."
JEREMIAH 31:3 NIV

The Lord is faithful;
He will strengthen you and
guard you from the evil one.
2 THESSALONIANS 3:3 NLT

This is love: not that we loved
God, but that He loved us and
sent His Son as an atoning
sacrifice for our sins.
1 JOHN 4:10 NIV

Your unfailing love, O Lord,
is as vast as the heavens;
Your faithfulness reaches
beyond the clouds. Your
righteousness is like the
mighty mountains, Your
justice like the ocean depths.
You care for people and
animals alike, O Lord.
PSALM 36:5-6 NLT

Praise the Lord, all nations! Extol
Him, all peoples! For great is His
steadfast love toward us, and the
faithfulness of the Lord endures
forever. Praise the Lord!
PSALM 117:1-2 ESV

I will declare that Your love
stands firm forever, that
You have established
Your faithfulness
in heaven itself.
PSALM 89:2 NIV

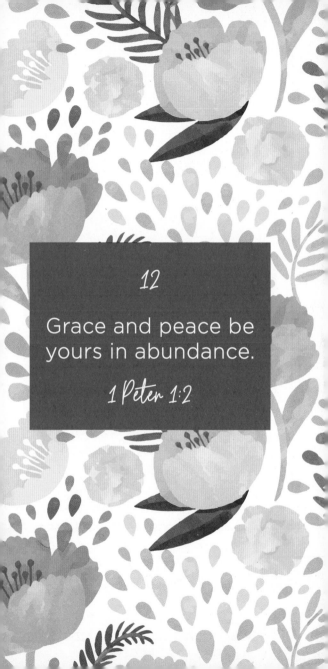

12

Grace and peace be yours in abundance.

1 Peter 1:2

We are all saved the same way,
by the undeserved grace
of the Lord Jesus.
ACTS 15:11 NLT

"My grace is sufficient for you,
for My power is made
perfect in weakness."
2 CORINTHIANS 12:9 ESV

Let us then approach God's throne
of grace with confidence, so that we
may receive mercy and find grace to
help us in our time of need.
HEBREWS 4:16 NIV

God is able to make all grace abound
to you, so that having all sufficiency
in all things at all times, you may
abound in every good work.
2 CORINTHIANS 9:8 ESV

Through Him we have also
obtained access by faith into this
grace in which we stand,
and we rejoice in hope
of the glory of God.
ROMANS 5:2 ESV

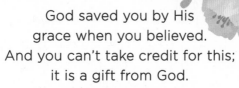

God saved you by His
grace when you believed.
And you can't take credit for this;
it is a gift from God.
EPHESIANS 2:8 NLT

From His abundance we
have all received one
gracious blessing after another.
JOHN 1:16 NLT

The LORD is compassionate
and gracious, slow to anger,
abounding in love.
PSALM 103:8 NIV

We praise God for the glorious
grace He has poured out on us
who belong to His dear Son.
EPHESIANS 1:6 NLT

For the grace of God has appeared,
bringing salvation for all people.
TITUS 2:11 ESV

To each one of us grace has been
given as Christ apportioned it.
EPHESIANS 4:7 NIV

May you experience the love
of Christ, though it is too great
to understand fully. Then you
will be made complete with
all the fullness of life and power
that comes from God.
EPHESIANS 3:19 NLT

The God of all grace, who
called you to His eternal glory
in Christ, after you have suffered
a little while, will Himself restore
you and make you strong,
firm and steadfast.
1 PETER 5:10 NIV

Even before I was born,
God chose me and called me
by His marvelous grace.
GALATIANS 1:15 NLT

The LORD will give grace and
glory; no good thing will
He withhold from those
who walk uprightly.
PSALM 84:11 NKJV

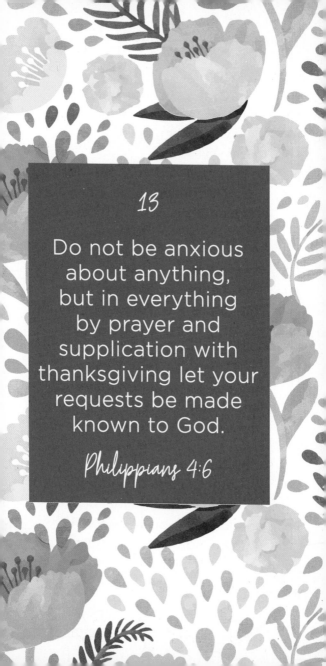

13

Do not be anxious about anything, but in everything by prayer and supplication with thanksgiving let your requests be made known to God.

Philippians 4:6

Cast all your anxiety on
Him because He cares for you.
1 PETER 5:7 NIV

Be strong, and do not fear, for your
God is coming to destroy your
enemies. He is coming to save you.
ISAIAH 35:4 NLT

The LORD is my light and my
salvation; whom shall I fear?
The LORD is the strength of my life;
of whom shall I be afraid?
PSALM 27:1 NKJV

I have set the LORD always
before me; because He is at my
right hand, I shall not be shaken.
PSALM 16:8 ESV

Do not be afraid and do not
panic before them. For the
LORD your God will personally
go ahead of you. He will neither
fail you nor abandon you.
DEUTERONOMY 31:6 NLT

Do not be afraid or discouraged, for the LORD will personally go ahead of you. He will be with you; He will neither fail you nor abandon you.

DEUTERONOMY 31:8 NLT

"So do not fear, for I am with you; do not be dismayed, for I am your God."

ISAIAH 41:10 NIV

"Do not be anxious about how you should defend yourself or what you should say, for the Holy Spirit will teach you in that very hour what you ought to say."

LUKE 12:11-12 ESV

You will keep in perfect peace all who trust in You, all whose thoughts are fixed on You! Trust in the LORD always, for the LORD GOD is the eternal Rock.

ISAIAH 26:3-4 NLT

"Be still, and know that I am God."

PSALM 46:10 ESV

Commit everything you
do to the LORD. Trust Him,
and He will help you.
PSALM 37:5 NLT

"Fear not, for I have
redeemed you; I have
called you by your name;
you are Mine."
ISAIAH 43:1 NKJV

When I am afraid,
I will put my trust in You.
PSALM 56:3 NLT

"Therefore do not be
anxious about tomorrow,
for tomorrow will be anxious
for itself. Sufficient for
the day is its own trouble."
MATTHEW 6:34 ESV

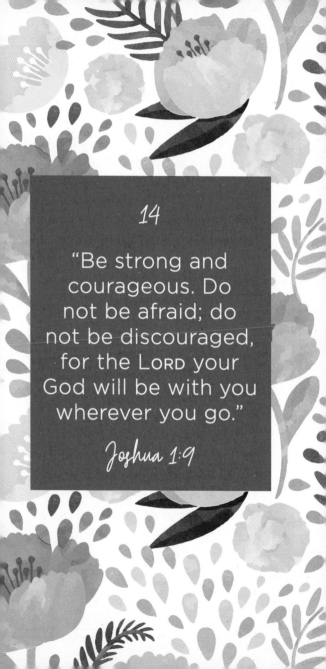

14

"Be strong and courageous. Do not be afraid; do not be discouraged, for the LORD your God will be with you wherever you go."

Joshua 1:9

"Where two or three are
gathered together in My name,
I am there in the midst of them."
MATTHEW 18:20 NKJV

"Anyone who loves Me will obey
My teaching. My Father will love
them, and We will come to them
and make Our home with them.
JOHN 14:23 NIV

Surely Your goodness and unfailing
love will pursue me all the days
of my life, and I will live in
the house of the LORD forever.
PSALM 23:6 NLT

The LORD your God is with you, the
Mighty Warrior who saves. He will
take great delight in you; in His love
He will no longer rebuke you, but will
rejoice over you with singing.
ZEPHANIAH 3:17 NIV

"Can anyone hide from Me in a secret place? Am I not everywhere in all the heavens and earth?" says the LORD.
JEREMIAH 23:24 NLT

For this is what the high and exalted One says – He who lives forever, whose name is holy: "I live in a high and holy place, but also with the one who is contrite and lowly in spirit, to revive the spirit of the lowly and to revive the heart of the contrite."
ISAIAH 57:15 NIV

The eyes of the LORD are in every place, keeping watch on the evil and the good.
PROVERBS 15:3 NKJV

God watches how people live; He sees everything they do.
JOB 34:21 NLT

"I will be your God throughout your lifetime – until your hair is white with age. I made you and I will care for you. I will carry you along and save you."
ISAIAH 46:4 NLT

He is before all things, and in Him all things hold together.
COLOSSIANS 1:17 ESV

"If you look for Me wholeheartedly, you will find Me."
JEREMIAH 29:13 NLT

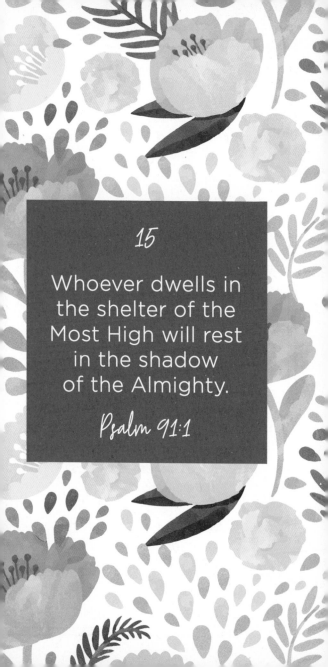

15

Whoever dwells in
the shelter of the
Most High will rest
in the shadow
of the Almighty.

Psalm 91:1

The Lord replied, "My Presence will go with you, and I will give you rest."
EXODUS 33:14 NIV

Jesus said, "Come to Me, all of you who are weary and carry heavy burdens, and I will give you rest."
MATTHEW 11:28 NLT

He said to them, "Come away by yourselves to a desolate place and rest a while."
MARK 6:31 ESV

Rest in the Lord, and wait patiently for Him; do not fret because of him who prospers in his way, because of the man who brings wicked schemes to pass.
PSALM 37:7 NKJV

In peace I will lie down and sleep, for You alone, O Lord, will keep me safe.
PSALM 4:8 NLT

The fear of the Lord leads to life;
then one rests content,
untouched by trouble.
PROVERBS 19:23 NIV

"Peace I leave with you; My peace I
give you. I do not give to you as the
world gives. Do not let your hearts
be troubled and do not be afraid."
JOHN 14:27 NIV

"I have told you all this so that
you may have peace in Me. Here on
earth you will have many trials and
sorrows. But take heart, because I
have overcome the world."
JOHN 16:33 NLT

The Lord gives strength to His
people; the Lord blesses His
people with peace.
PSALM 29:11 NIV

Great peace have those who
love Your law, and nothing
can make them stumble.
PSALM 119:165 NIV

Let the peace of Christ
rule in your hearts.
COLOSSIANS 3:15 ESV

You will keep in perfect peace
those whose minds are steadfast,
because they trust in You.
ISAIAH 26:3 NIV

God is not a God of
confusion but of peace.
1 CORINTHIANS 14:33 ESV

The God of peace
be with you.
ROMANS 15:33 NIV

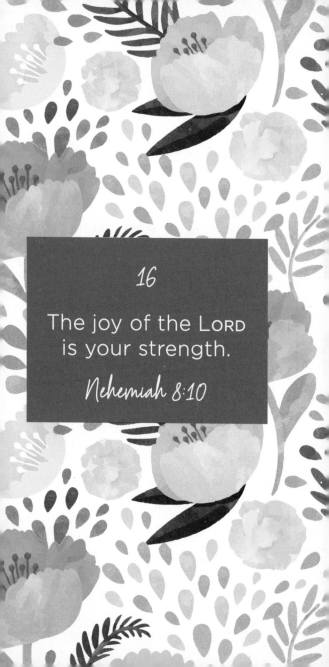

16

The joy of the LORD
is your strength.

Nehemiah 8:10

This is the day that the LORD has made; let us rejoice and be glad in it.
PSALM 118:24 ESV

Those who sow with tears will reap with songs of joy.
PSALM 126:5 NIV

The LORD is my strength and song, and He has become my salvation.
PSALM 118:14 NKJV

Glory in His holy name; let the hearts of those who seek the LORD rejoice.
PSALM 105:3 NIV

"Rejoice because your names are written in heaven."
LUKE 10:20 NKJV

"Be happy! Yes, leap for joy! For a great reward awaits you in heaven."
LUKE 6:23 NLT

Honor and majesty are before Him; strength and gladness are in His place.
1 CHRONICLES 16:27 NKJV

You turned my wailing into dancing; You removed my sackcloth and clothed me with joy.

PSALM 30:11 NIV

Those who look to Him for help will be radiant with joy; no shadow of shame will darken their faces.

PSALM 34:5 NLT

Because You are my help, I sing in the shadow of Your wings.

PSALM 63:7 NIV

You have given me greater joy than those who have abundant harvests of grain and new wine.

PSALM 4:7 NLT

The precepts of the LORD are right, giving joy to the heart.
The commands of the LORD are radiant, giving light to the eyes.

PSALM 19:8 NIV

In Him our hearts rejoice, for we trust in His holy name.

PSALM 33:21 NIV

Let all those who seek You
rejoice and be glad in You;
and let those who love Your
salvation say continually,
"Let God be magnified!"
PSALM 70:4 NKJV

For His anger lasts only a
moment, but His favor lasts
a lifetime; weeping may
stay for the night,
but rejoicing comes
in the morning.
PSALM 30:5 NIV

Light shines on the godly,
and joy on those whose
hearts are right.
PSALM 97:11 NLT

The Lord has done
great things for us,
and we are filled
with joy.
PSALM 126:3 NIV

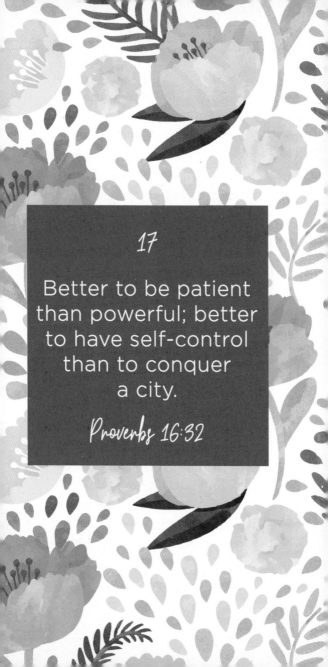

17

Better to be patient than powerful; better to have self-control than to conquer a city.

Proverbs 16:32

Be joyful in hope, patient in
affliction, faithful in prayer.
ROMANS 12:12 NIV

I waited patiently for the LORD; He
turned to me and heard my cry.
PSALM 40:1 NIV

Wait for the LORD; be strong and
take heart and wait for the LORD.
PSALM 27:14 NIV

The end of a matter is better
than its beginning, and patience
is better than pride.
ECCLESIASTES 7:8 NIV

Through patience a ruler can
be persuaded, and a gentle
tongue can break a bone.
PROVERBS 25:15 NIV

If we look forward to something we
don't yet have, we must wait
patiently and confidently.
ROMANS 8:25 NLT

You, Lord, are a compassionate
and gracious God, slow to anger,
abounding in love and faithfulness.
PSALM 86:15 NIV

As the elect of God, holy and
beloved, put on tender
mercies, kindness, humility,
meekness, longsuffering.
COLOSSIANS 3:12 NKJV

Be completely humble and gentle;
be patient, bearing with one
another in love. Make every effort
to keep the unity of the Spirit
through the bond of peace.
EPHESIANS 4:2-3 NIV

Be still before the Lord and
wait patiently for Him; do not
fret when people succeed in their
ways, when they carry out their
wicked schemes. Refrain from
anger and turn from wrath.
PSALM 37:7-8 NIV

The Lord is not slow in keeping
His promise, as some understand
slowness. Instead He is patient
with you, not wanting anyone
to perish, but everyone
to come to repentance.
2 PETER 3:9 NIV

You need to persevere so
that when you have done the
will of God, you will receive
what He has promised.
HEBREWS 10:36 NIV

It is good that one should
wait quietly for the
salvation of the LORD.
LAMENTATIONS 3:26 ESV

Hope that is seen is no hope
at all. Who hopes for
what they already have?
ROMANS 8:24 NIV

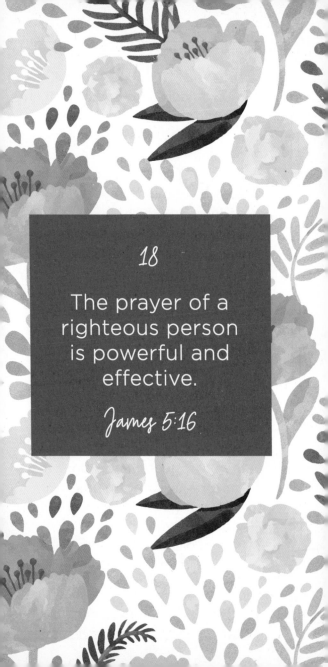

18

The prayer of a
righteous person
is powerful and
effective.

James 5:16

Devote yourselves to prayer with an alert mind and a thankful heart.
COLOSSIANS 4:2 NLT

Pray in the Spirit on all occasions with all kinds of prayers and requests. With this in mind, be alert and always keep on praying for all the Lord's people.
EPHESIANS 6:18 NIV

Let my prayer be set before You as incense, the lifting up of my hands as the evening sacrifice.
PSALM 141:2 NKJV

When you pray, go into your room, close the door and pray to your Father, who is unseen. Then your Father, who sees what is done in secret, will reward you.
MATTHEW 6:6 NIV

The LORD delights in the prayers of the upright.
PROVERBS 15:8 NLT

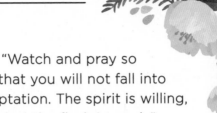

"Watch and pray so
that you will not fall into
temptation. The spirit is willing,
but the flesh is weak."
MATTHEW 26:41 NIV

Give ear, O LORD, to my prayer;
listen to my plea for grace.
PSALM 86:6 ESV

Is anyone among you in trouble?
Let them pray. Is anyone happy?
Let them sing songs of praise.
JAMES 5:13 NIV

I confessed all my sins to You
and stopped trying to hide my
guilt. I said to myself, "I will confess
my rebellion to the LORD." And You
forgave me! All my guilt is gone.
Therefore, let all the godly pray
to You while there is still time,
that they may not drown in the
floodwaters of judgment.
PSALM 32:5-6 NLT

"If you believe, you will receive whatever you ask for in prayer."
MATTHEW 21:22 NIV

This is the confidence that we have in Him, that if we ask anything according to His will, He hears us. And if we know that He hears us, whatever we ask, we know that we have the petitions that we have asked of Him.
1 JOHN 5:14-15 NKJV

The eyes of the Lord are on the righteous and His ears are attentive to their prayer.
1 PETER 3:12 NIV

"I tell you, you can pray for anything, and if you believe that you've received it, it will be yours."
MARK 11:24 NLT

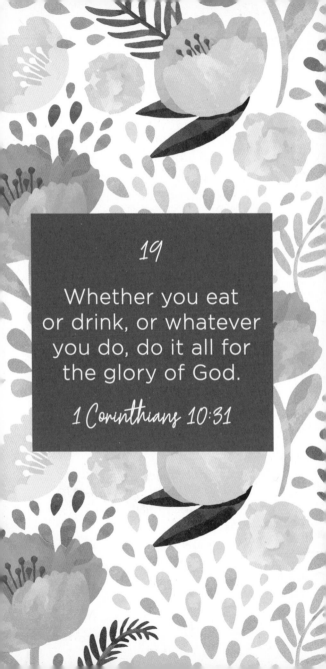

19

Whether you eat
or drink, or whatever
you do, do it all for
the glory of God.

1 Corinthians 10:31

The Lord your God will bless
you in all your harvest and in
all the work of your hands,
and your joy will be complete.
DEUTERONOMY 16:15 NIV

"Be strong, all you people of the
land," says the Lord, "and work; for I
am with you," says the Lord of hosts.
HAGGAI 2:4 NKJV

You shall eat the fruit of the labor
of your hands; you shall be blessed,
and it shall be well with you.
PSALM 128:2 ESV

Whatever you do, in word or deed,
do everything in the name of the
Lord Jesus, giving thanks to
God the Father through Him.
COLOSSIANS 3:17 ESV

Work hard and become a leader;
be lazy and become a slave.
PROVERBS 12:24 NLT

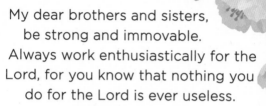

My dear brothers and sisters,
be strong and immovable.
Always work enthusiastically for the
Lord, for you know that nothing you
do for the Lord is ever useless.
1 CORINTHIANS 15:58 NLT

Let the favor of the Lord our God
be upon us, and establish the
work of our hands upon us; yes,
establish the work of our hands!
PSALM 90:17 ESV

Work brings profit, but mere
talk leads to poverty! Wealth is a
crown for the wise; the effort of
fools yields only foolishness.
PROVERBS 14:23-24 NLT

Lazy people want much but
get little, but those who
work hard will prosper.
PROVERBS 13:4 NLT

I can do all things through Christ
who strengthens me.
PHILIPPIANS 4:13 NKJV

A hard worker has plenty of food, but a person who chases fantasies has no sense.
PROVERBS 12:11 NLT

"Do not labor for the food which perishes, but for the food which endures to everlasting life, which the Son of Man will give you, because God the Father has set His seal on Him."
JOHN 6:27 NKJV

There is nothing better than to enjoy food and drink and to find satisfaction in work ... these pleasures are from the hand of God.
ECCLESIASTES 2:24 NLT

From the fruit of their lips people are filled with good things, and the work of their hands brings them reward.
PROVERBS 12:14 NIV

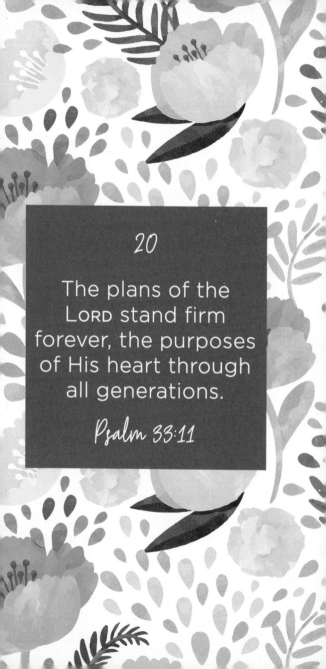

20

The plans of the
LORD stand firm
forever, the purposes
of His heart through
all generations.

Psalm 33:11

"Before I formed you in the womb I knew you, and before you were born I consecrated you; I appointed you a prophet to the nations."

JEREMIAH 1:4-5 ESV

You made all the delicate, inner parts of my body and knit me together in my mother's womb. Thank You for making me so wonderfully complex! Your workmanship is marvelous – how well I know it.

PSALM 139:13-14 NLT

For we are God's masterpiece. He has created us anew in Christ Jesus, so we can do the good things He planned for us long ago.

EPHESIANS 2:10 NLT

God created mankind in His own image, in the image of God He created them; male and female He created them.

GENESIS 1:27 NIV

Know that the Lord, He is God!
It is He who made us, and we
are His; we are His people,
and the sheep of His pasture.
PSALM 100:3 ESV

Even before He made the world,
God loved us and chose us in
Christ to be holy and without
fault in His eyes. God decided
in advance to adopt us into His
own family by bringing us to
Himself through Jesus Christ.
EPHESIANS 1:4-5 NLT

The Spirit of God has made me; the
breath of the Almighty gives me life.
JOB 33:4 NIV

"You didn't choose Me. I chose
you. I appointed you to go and
produce lasting fruit, so that the
Father will give you whatever you
ask for, using My name."
JOHN 15:16 NLT

In Him also we have
obtained an inheritance, being
predestined according to the
purpose of Him who works
all things according to the
counsel of His will, that we who
first trusted in Christ should
be to the praise of His glory.
EPHESIANS 1:11-12 NKJV

Many are the plans in a
person's heart, but it is the
LORD's purpose that prevails.
PROVERBS 19:21 NIV

All the days ordained for
me were written in Your book
before one of them came to be.
PSALM 139:16 NIV

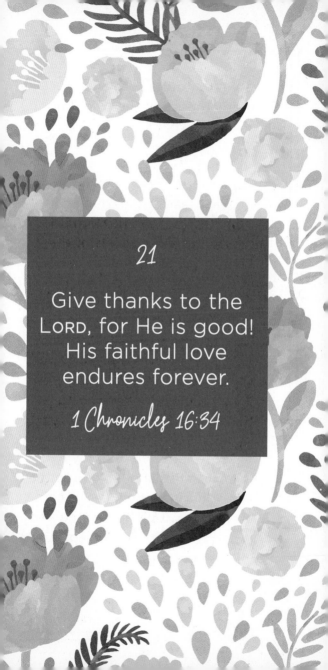

21

Give thanks to the
LORD, for He is good!
His faithful love
endures forever.

1 Chronicles 16:34

Give thanks to the LORD and proclaim His greatness. Let the whole world know what He has done.
PSALM 105:1 NLT

Thanks be to God, who in Christ always leads us in triumphal procession, and through us spreads the fragrance of the knowledge of Him everywhere.
2 CORINTHIANS 2:14 ESV

It is good to give thanks to the LORD, to sing praises to the Most High. It is good to proclaim Your unfailing love in the morning, Your faithfulness in the evening.
PSALM 92:1-2 NLT

Come, let us sing for joy to the LORD; let us shout aloud to the Rock of our salvation. Let us come before Him with thanksgiving and extol Him with music and song. For the LORD is the great God, the great King above all gods.
PSALM 95:1-3 NIV

Enter His gates with thanksgiving and His courts with praise; give thanks to Him and praise His name.
PSALM 100:4 NIV

Thank God! He gives us victory over sin and death through our Lord Jesus Christ.
1 CORINTHIANS 15:57 NLT

Oh give thanks to the LORD; call upon His name; make known His deeds among the peoples!
1 CHRONICLES 16:8 ESV

We give thanks to You, O God, we give thanks! For Your wondrous works declare that Your name is near.
PSALM 75:1 NKJV

May you be filled with joy, always thanking the Father.
COLOSSIANS 1:11-12 NLT

I will give thanks to the LORD with my whole heart; I will recount all of Your wonderful deeds. I will be glad and exult in You; I will sing praise to Your name, O Most High.

PSALM 9:1-2 ESV

Sing and make music from your heart to the Lord, always giving thanks to God the Father for everything, in the name of our Lord Jesus Christ.

EPHESIANS 5:19-20 NIV

Whatever you do, in word or deed, do everything in the name of the Lord Jesus, giving thanks to God the Father through Him.

COLOSSIANS 3:17 ESV

22

The LORD will guide you always; He will satisfy your needs in a sun-scorched land and will strengthen your frame.

Isaiah 58:11

Show me Your ways, LORD, teach
me Your paths. Guide me in
Your truth and teach me, for
You are God my Savior, and
my hope is in You all day long.
PSALM 25:4-5 NIV

Send out Your light and Your
truth; let them guide me. Let them
lead me to Your holy mountain,
to the place where You live.
PSALM 43:3 NLT

"Call to Me, and I will answer you,
and show you great and mighty
things, which you do not know."
JEREMIAH 33:3 NKJV

Your word is a lamp to guide
my feet and a light for my path.
PSALM 119:105 NLT

Teach me to do Your will, for You
are my God! Let Your good
Spirit lead me on level ground!
PSALM 143:10 ESV

The Lᴏʀᴅ directs the steps
of the godly. He delights in
every detail of their lives.
PSALM 37:23 NLT

Whether you turn to the right
or to the left, your ears will hear
a voice behind you, saying,
"This is the way; walk in it."
ISAIAH 30:21 NIV

Direct my steps by Your word,
and let no iniquity have
dominion over me.
PSALM 119:133 NKJV

All who are led by the Spirit
of God are children of God.
ROMANS 8:14 NLT

"I will go before you and make the
crooked places straight; I will break
in pieces the gates of bronze
and cut the bars of iron."
ISAIAH 45:2 NKJV

He guides the humble in what is
right and teaches them His way.
PSALM 25:9 NIV

The LORD is good and does
what is right; He shows the proper
path to those who go astray.
PSALM 25:8 NLT

God is our God for
ever and ever; He will be
our guide even to the end.
PSALM 48:14 NIV

The LORD says, "I will guide you
along the best pathway for
your life. I will advise you
and watch over you."
PSALM 32:8 NLT

May He give you the desire
of your heart and make all
your plans succeed.
PSALM 20:4 NIV

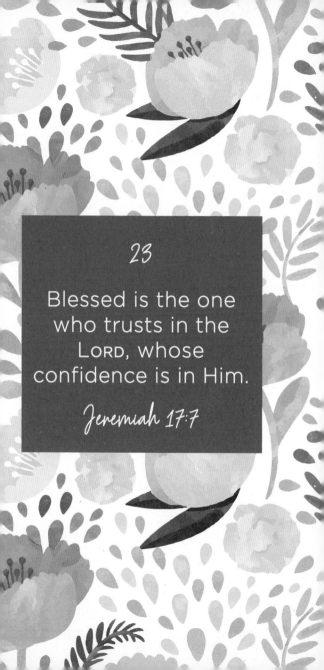

23

Blessed is the one
who trusts in the
LORD, whose
confidence is in Him.

Jeremiah 17:7

Blessed are those whose
way is blameless, who
walk in the law of the Lord!
PSALM 119:1 ESV

"God blesses those who are poor
and realize their need for Him, for
the Kingdom of Heaven is theirs."
MATTHEW 5:3 NLT

Oh, taste and see that the
Lord is good; blessed is the
man who trusts in Him!
PSALM 34:8 NKJV

The Lord will indeed give
what is good, and our land
will yield its harvest.
PSALM 85:12 NIV

Blessed are the pure in heart,
for they shall see God."
MATTHEW 5:8 NKJV

The blessing of the Lord
brings wealth, without
painful toil for it.
PROVERBS 10:22 NIV

When You open Your hand,
You satisfy the hunger and thirst
of every living thing. The Lord is
righteous in everything He does;
He is filled with kindness.
PSALM 145:16-17 NLT

The Lord bless you and keep you;
the Lord make His face shine upon
you, and be gracious to you; the
Lord lift up His countenance upon
you, and give you peace.
NUMBERS 6:24-26 NKJV

The Lord is my chosen portion and
my cup; You hold my lot. The lines
have fallen for me in pleasant places;
indeed, I have a beautiful inheritance.
PSALM 16:5-6 ESV

"I will bless those who have
humble and contrite hearts,
who tremble at My word."
ISAIAH 66:2 NLT

"God blesses those who
are merciful, for they
will be shown mercy."
MATTHEW 5:7 NLT

All praise to God, the Father
of our Lord Jesus Christ, who
has blessed us with every
spiritual blessing in the
heavenly realms because
we are united with Christ.
EPHESIANS 1:3 NLT

"Blessed are the meek,
for they will inherit the earth."
MATTHEW 5:5 NIV

You go before me and follow
me. You place Your hand of
blessing on my head. Such
knowledge is too wonderful
for me, too great for
me to understand!
PSALM 139:5-6 NLT

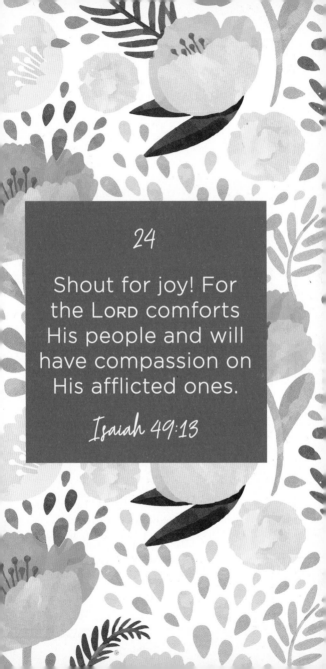

24

Shout for joy! For the LORD comforts His people and will have compassion on His afflicted ones.

Isaiah 49:13

The LORD will not reject His
people; He will not abandon
His special possession.
PSALM 94:14 NLT

He heals the brokenhearted
and binds up their wounds.
PSALM 147:3 NIV

Let Your unfailing love comfort me,
just as You promised me.
PSALM 119:76 NLT

"Blessed are those who mourn,
for they will be comforted."
MATTHEW 5:4 NIV

"I, yes I, am the one who comforts
you. So why are you afraid?"
ISAIAH 51:12 NLT

We know that in
all things God works
for the good of those
who love Him.
ROMANS 8:28 NIV

Though I walk in the midst of trouble, You preserve my life; You stretch out Your hand against the wrath of my enemies, and Your right hand delivers me.

PSALM 138:7 ESV

As the deer longs for streams of water, so I long for You, O God. I thirst for God, the living God. When can I go and stand before Him?

PSALM 42:1 NLT

The LORD upholds all who fall, and raises up all who are bowed down.

PSALM 145:14 NKJV

Come, let us bow down in worship, let us kneel before the LORD our Maker; for He is our God and we are the people of His pasture, the flock under His care.

PSALM 95:6-7 NIV

The LORD is close to the brokenhearted; He rescues those whose spirits are crushed.

PSALM 34:18 NLT

"See, I have engraved you on the palms of My hands; your walls are ever before Me."
ISAIAH 49:16 NIV

Weeping may endure for a night, but joy comes in the morning.
PSALM 30:5 NKJV

Praise be to the God and Father of our Lord Jesus Christ, the Father of compassion and the God of all comfort, who comforts us in all our troubles.
2 CORINTHIANS 1:3-4 NIV

Aim for restoration, comfort one another, agree with one another, live in peace; and the God of love and peace will be with you.
2 CORINTHIANS 13:11 ESV

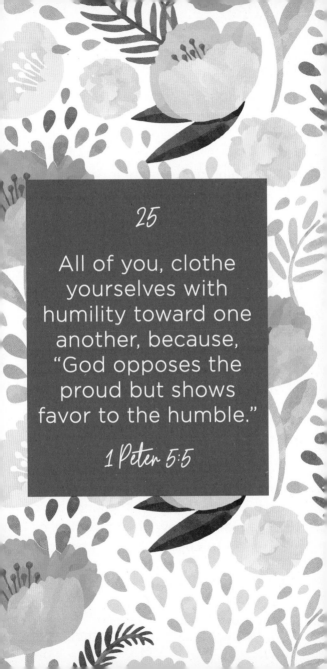

25

All of you, clothe yourselves with humility toward one another, because, "God opposes the proud but shows favor to the humble."

1 Peter 5:5

Humble yourselves in the sight of
the Lord, and He will lift you up.
JAMES 4:10 NKJV

True humility and fear of the LORD
lead to riches, honor, and long life.
PROVERBS 22:4 NLT

"I will bless those who have
humble and contrite hearts,
who tremble at My word."
ISAIAH 66:2 NLT

"He who is greatest among you shall
be your servant. And whoever exalts
himself will be humbled, and he who
humbles himself will be exalted."
MATTHEW 23:11-12 NKJV

"Truly, I say to you, unless you
turn and become like children,
you will never enter the kingdom of
heaven. Whoever humbles himself
like this child is the greatest in the
kingdom of heaven."
MATTHEW 18:3-4 ESV

Pride leads to disgrace,
but with humility comes wisdom.
PROVERBS 11:2 NLT

He has shown you, O mortal,
what is good. And what does the
Lord require of you? To act justly
and to love mercy and to walk
humbly with your God.
MICAH 6:8 NIV

A man's pride will bring him low, but
the humble in spirit will retain honor.
PROVERBS 29:23 NKJV

The meek will inherit the land and
enjoy peace and prosperity.
PSALM 37:11 NIV

Be like-minded,
be sympathetic,
love one another,
be compassionate
and humble.
1 PETER 3:8 NIV

Do nothing out of selfish
ambition or vain conceit. Rather,
in humility value others above
yourselves, not looking to your
own interests but each of you to
the interests of the others.
PHILIPPIANS 2:3-4 NIV

The LORD supports the humble,
but He brings the wicked
down into the dust.
PSALM 147:6 NLT

"Blessed are the poor
in spirit, for theirs is
the kingdom of heaven."
MATTHEW 5:3 NKJV

Haughtiness goes before
destruction; humility
precedes honor.
PROVERBS 18:12 NLT

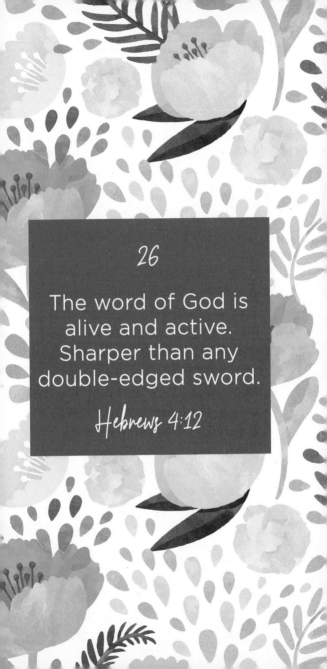

26

The word of God is
alive and active.
Sharper than any
double-edged sword.

Hebrews 4:12

All Scripture is inspired by God
and is useful to teach us what is
true and to make us realize what is
wrong in our lives. It corrects
us when we are wrong and teaches
us to do what is right. God uses
it to prepare and equip His people
to do every good work.

2 TIMOTHY 3:16-17 NLT

Don't just listen to God's word.
You must do what it says. Otherwise,
you are only fooling yourselves.
For if you listen to the word and
don't obey, it is like glancing at your
face in a mirror. You see yourself,
walk away, and forget what you look
like. But if you look carefully into the
perfect law that sets you free, and
if you do what it says and don't
forget what you heard, then
God will bless you for doing it.

JAMES 1:22-25 NLT

"Blessed rather are those
who hear the word of
God and obey it."

LUKE 11:28 NIV

Jesus answered, "It is written:
'Man shall not live on bread alone,
but on every word that comes
from the mouth of God.'"
MATTHEW 4:4 NIV

For whatever was written in former
days was written for our instruction,
that through endurance and
through the encouragement of the
Scriptures we might have hope.
ROMANS 15:4 ESV

"Keep this Book of the Law
always on your lips; meditate
on it day and night, so that you
may be careful to do everything
written in it. Then you will be
prosperous and successful."
JOSHUA 1:8 NIV

"Heaven and earth will pass away,
but My words will never pass away."
MATTHEW 24:35 NIV

Your word, LORD, is eternal;
it stands firm in the heavens.
PSALM 119:89 NIV

Blessed are those whose way is
blameless, who walk in the law
of the LORD! Blessed are those
who keep His testimonies,
who seek Him with their whole
heart, who also do no wrong,
but walk in His ways!
PSALM 119:1-3 ESV

In the beginning was the Word,
and the Word was with God,
and the Word was God.
JOHN 1:1 ESV

The Word became flesh and made
His dwelling among us. We have
seen His glory, the glory
of the one and only Son,
who came from the Father,
full of grace and truth.
JOHN 1:14 NIV

27

Set your minds on things above, not on earthly things.

Colossians 3:2

Whoever has the Son has life;
whoever does not have the Son
of God does not have life.
1 JOHN 5:12 ESV

"My Father's will is that everyone
who looks to the Son and believes
in Him shall have eternal life."
JOHN 6:40 NIV

"I give them eternal life, and they
shall never perish; no one will snatch
them out of My hand. My Father,
who has given them to Me,
is greater than all; no one can
snatch them out of My Father's
hand. I and the Father are one."
JOHN 10:28-30 NIV

For the wages of sin is death, but
the free gift of God is eternal life
through Christ Jesus our Lord.
ROMANS 6:23 NLT

He who believes in the Son has everlasting life; and he who does not believe the Son shall not see life, but the wrath of God abides on him.

JOHN 3:36 NKJV

"You can enter God's Kingdom only through the narrow gate. The highway to hell is broad, and its gate is wide for the many who choose that way. But the gateway to life is very narrow and the road is difficult, and only a few ever find it."

MATTHEW 7:13-14 NLT

"Whoever drinks of this water will thirst again, but whoever drinks of the water that I shall give him will never thirst. But the water that I shall give him will become in him a fountain of water springing up into everlasting life."

JOHN 4:13-14 NKJV

"Everyone who lives in Me and
believes in Me will never ever die."
JOHN 11:26 NLT

"Father, the hour has come.
Glorify Your Son, that Your Son
may glorify You. For You granted
Him authority over all people
that He might give eternal life to
all those You have given Him.
Now this is eternal life: that
they know You, the only
true God, and Jesus Christ,
whom You have sent."
JOHN 17:1-3 NIV

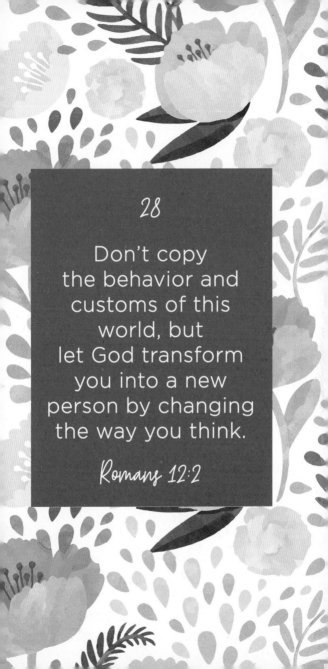

28

Don't copy
the behavior and
customs of this
world, but
let God transform
you into a new
person by changing
the way you think.

Romans 12:2

Put on your new nature, and be
renewed as you learn to know your
Creator and become like Him.
COLOSSIANS 3:10 NLT

If anyone is in Christ, the
new creation has come: The
old has gone, the new is here!
2 CORINTHIANS 5:17 NIV

You were taught, with regard to
your former way of life, to put
off your old self, which is being
corrupted by its deceitful desires;
to be made new in the attitude of
your minds; and to put on the new
self, created to be like God in true
righteousness and holiness.
EPHESIANS 4:22-24 NIV

Do not let sin control the way
you live. Instead, give yourselves
completely to God, for you were
dead, but now you have new life.
ROMANS 6:12-13 NLT

No temptation has overtaken you that is not common to man. God is faithful, and He will not let you be tempted beyond your ability, but with the temptation He will also provide the way of escape, that you may be able to endure it.
1 CORINTHIANS 10:13 ESV

Make it your goal to live a quiet life, minding your own business and working with your hands, just as we instructed you before.
1 THESSALONIANS 4:11 NLT

When He died, He died once to break the power of sin. But now that He lives, He lives for the glory of God. So you also should consider yourselves to be dead to the power of sin and alive to God through Christ Jesus.
ROMANS 6:10-11 NLT

Submit yourselves, then, to God.
Resist the devil, and he
will flee from you.
JAMES 4:7 NIV

The night is almost gone; the
day of salvation will soon be here.
So remove your dark deeds
like dirty clothes, and put on the
shining armor of right living.
ROMANS 13:12 NLT

Prove by the way you live that
you have repented of your
sins and turned to God.
MATTHEW 3:8 NLT

29

Draw near to God,
and He will draw
near to you.

James 4:8

Those who know Your name will put their trust in You; for You, Lord, have not forsaken those who seek You.

PSALM 9:10 NKJV

My heart says of You, "Seek His face!" Your face, Lord, I will seek. Do not hide Your face from me, do not turn Your servant away in anger; You have been my helper.

PSALM 27:8-9 NIV

Seek the Lord your God, and you will find Him if you seek Him with all your heart and with all your soul.

DEUTERONOMY 4:29 NKJV

"Ask, and it will be given to you; seek, and you will find; knock, and it will be opened to you. For everyone who asks receives, and the one who seeks finds, and to the one who knocks it will be opened."

MATTHEW 7:7-8 ESV

Seek the LORD and His
strength; seek His
face evermore!
PSALM 105:4 NKJV

The LORD looks down from heaven
on all mankind to see if there are any
who understand, any who seek God.
PSALM 14:2 NIV

The LORD is with you while you
are with Him. If you seek Him,
He will be found by you.
2 CHRONICLES 15:2 ESV

The lions may grow weak and
hungry, but those who seek
the LORD lack no good thing.
PSALM 34:10 NIV

The LORD sees every heart and
knows every plan and thought.
If you seek Him, you will find Him.
But if you forsake Him,
He will reject you forever.
1 CHRONICLES 28:9 NLT

Devote your heart and soul to
seeking the LORD your God.
1 CHRONICLES 22:19 NIV

"Seek the Kingdom of God
above all else, and live
righteously, and He will give
you everything you need."
MATTHEW 6:33 NLT

You, God, are my God,
earnestly I seek You.
PSALM 63:1 NIV

Seek the LORD while He may
be found; call upon Him
while He is near.
ISAIAH 55:6 ESV

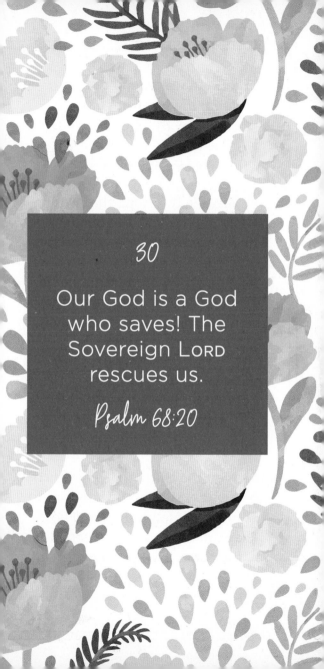

30

Our God is a God
who saves! The
Sovereign Lᴏʀᴅ
rescues us.

Psalm 68:20

In Him we have redemption through His blood, the forgiveness of sins, in accordance with the riches of God's grace that He lavished on us.

EPHESIANS 1:7-8 NIV

Jesus is the stone that was rejected by you, the builders, which has become the cornerstone. And there is salvation in no one else, for there is no other name under heaven given among men by which we must be saved.

ACTS 4:11-12 ESV

The LORD takes pleasure in His people; He will beautify the humble with salvation.

PSALM 149:4 NKJV

"I tell you the truth, those who listen to My message and believe in God who sent Me have eternal life. They will never be condemned for their sins, but they have already passed from death into life."

JOHN 5:24 NLT

"My sheep hear My voice, and I know them, and they follow Me. And I give them eternal life, and they shall never perish; neither shall anyone snatch them out of My hand. My Father, who has given them to Me, is greater than all; and no one is able to snatch them out of My Father's hand."

JOHN 10:27-29 NKJV

I delight greatly in the LORD; my soul rejoices in my God. For He has clothed me with garments of salvation and arrayed me in a robe of righteousness.

ISAIAH 61:10 NIV

It is good that one should hope and wait quietly for the salvation of the LORD.

LAMENTATIONS 3:26 NKJV

Restore to me the joy of Your salvation and grant me a willing spirit, to sustain me.

PSALM 51:12 NIV

Believe in the Lord Jesus,
and you will be saved,
you and your household.
ACTS 16:31 ESV

If you openly declare that Jesus is
Lord and believe in your heart that
God raised Him from the dead, you
will be saved. For it is by believing in
your heart that you are made right
with God, and it is by openly
declaring your faith that
you are saved.
ROMANS 10:9-10 NLT

For there is no distinction
between Jew and Greek, for the
same Lord over all is rich to all who
call upon Him. For "whoever calls on
the name of the LORD shall be saved."
ROMANS 10:12-13 NKJV

He is able to save to the uttermost those who draw near to God through Him, since He always lives to make intercession for them.
HEBREWS 7:25 ESV

God says, "At just the right time, I heard you. On the day of salvation, I helped you." Indeed, the "right time" is now. Today is the day of salvation.
2 CORINTHIANS 6:2 NLT

If we walk in the light, as He is in the light, we have fellowship with one another, and the blood of Jesus His Son cleanses us from all sin.
1 JOHN 1:7 ESV